MARCHING AS TO WAR: THE BEGINNINGS OF FREEDOM IN SOUTH
CAROLINA
RECONSTRUCTION AND EDUCATION IN SOUTH CAROLINA:
CONTRIBUTIONS OF THE REVEREND BENJAMIN FRANKLIN
RANDOLPH, 1865-1868

A Thesis

by
William W. Cooper, Jr.

Atlanta, Georgia
2001

TABLE OF CONTENTS

RATIONALE FOR THESIS 4

STATEMENT OF PROBLEM 5

INTRODUCTION 7

REVIEW OF THE LITERATURE ..…………………………………………......12

METHOD …………………………………………………………………..…... 17

Section
1 THE EARLY EDUCATION OF BLACKS IN THE SOUTH 19
       Northerners and the Movement to Educate Blacks in South Carolina 21
       The Freedmen's Bureau in South Carolina..24
       Barriers that Affected the Development of South Carolina......................25
       The First Petition for a State System of Education 28

2 RANDOLPH AND BLACK CITIZENSHIP 30
       Benjamin Franklin Randolph 30
       Black Political Organization in South Carolina during Reconstruction ..31
       Randolph as Union Army Chaplain..32
       Randolph and the American Missionary Association..............................34
       The Colored People's Convention of South Carolina..............................35
       Randolph and Equality..38
       Blacks and Citizenship Rights 40
       The Reaction to Black Citizenship..42
       Corruption during Reconstruction 43
       Structural Change in South Carolina 46
       Blacks and Freedom..47

3 THE DEVELOPMENT OF A PUBLIC SYSTEM OF EDUCATION 50
       The 1868 Constitutional Convention 50
       The Educational Provision 52
       Article 10...54
       The Death of Benjamin Franklin Randolph 55
       Barriers that Affected the Educational Provision.....................................56
       Black Leadership during Reconstruction 58
       Black Legislators...59
       The Benefits of Reconstruction...62

    CONCLUSION 65

REFERENCES ………………………………………………………….67

DEDICATION

This text is dedicated to the many unnamed people that worked to build the foundation for change in the South. May this and other forgotten history be remembered, explored, and give it's proper place.

RATIONALE FOR THESIS

This thesis is the result of research on the life of the Rev. Benjamin Franklin Randolph and an examination of his work in South Carolina during Reconstruction. My interest in Randolph was two-fold. First, I, like Randolph, served as a military Chaplain. After reading a Chaplain's report written by Randolph, I was impressed by his emphasis on improving the moral and intellectual capacities of black soldiers and decided to do additional research on him. Second, my interest was sparked because Randolph served as a missionary and an educator in South Carolina, which became the foundation that allowed him to become a prominent black leader during Reconstruction.

As a native of South Carolina, I was intrigued by Randolph's significant participation in the Reconstruction of South Carolina. Although little is known about Randolph, this thesis proposes an analysis of his involvement at the 1868 Constitutional Convention, in which he played a vital role. The efforts of Randolph and other black officials led to the creation of South Carolina's first public school system. I also propose to consider the significance of blacks as elected officials.

As a product of South Carolina's public school system, the research on Randolph educated me on the role blacks played in reconstituting my home state and the inception of the first public school system without racial distinction.

STATEMENT OF THE PROBLEM

The South Carolina Constitutional Convention of 1868 was the first constitutional convention in South Carolina history in which blacks served as legislators. Additionally, for the first time in America blacks comprised the majority of a state house of representatives. Rev. Benjamin Franklin Randolph addressed the convention participants as a delegate, asserting equal treatment for blacks, and arguing for the establishment of a public education system. Other black delegates affirmed Randolph's concern for a formal system of education and they helped public education become a part of the constitution. In spite of this, the role of blacks in South Carolina during Reconstruction was believed to be insignificant. The problem that will be addressed in this thesis will highlight the discredited significance of black involvement in South Carolina during Reconstruction. In this thesis, I note that a constitutional provision for a state-supported public education system did not exist in South Carolina before Reconstruction. However, at the 1868 Constitutional Convention, the state legislature placed into law an educational provision mandating the equal access to education for both blacks and whites in South Carolina.

I propose that the South Carolina Constitutional Convention of 1868 was noteworthy for two interrelated reasons: (a) the significant participation of black legislators; and (b) the educational provision of the constitution that was introduced while blacks formed a majority in the lower house of the state legislature. It is argued that the educational provision, a petition led by Randolph, began the state's first public educational system without racial distinction.

Racial division quickly became a major barrier in South Carolina's development during Reconstruction. Blacks held majority power in the state legislature and were opposed by most whites because they were viewed as a group incapable of handling legislative power responsibly. The fact that black involvement in political affairs during Reconstruction was strongly opposed may begin to explain why the role of blacks has apparently been discredited. Du Bois (1935) discussed three misconceptions that were held about blacks and Reconstruction: (a) that blacks were ignorant; (b) that blacks were lazy, dishonest and extravagant; and (c) that blacks were responsible for bad government during Reconstruction (pp. 711-712). Du Bois theorized that these misconceptions led to the belief that blacks did not contribute positively or significantly during Reconstruction.

South Carolina's governmental structure during Reconstruction engendered significant legislation under the leadership of a majority black legislature. This historical occurrence gave birth to a state policy on suffrage, and the adoption of a state supported educational system, initiated by Randolph at the Constitutional Convention of 1868.

INTRODUCTION

By the early 1800s, slavery was an institution that had existed for at least a century in America. Slave labor was a primary physical resource used by the founders of the Republic to build the infrastructure and support the economic needs of the new country. The largely agrarian economy that early settlers established demanded immense physical labor, which was filled in large part by slaves. However, the northern part of the country had become more industrial by the early 1800s and eventually abandoned slavery. "The need for black labor may have been even greater in the South than in the North by this time. This was because the South produced such crops as cotton, tobacco, sugar and rice in large quantities" (Wesley, 1926, p. 3). Northern states such as New York were forerunners in establishing industrial economies. But southern states, such as Virginia, Louisiana and South Carolina, were neither willing to change the basis of their economic system nor to abandon slavery (Wesley, 1926, p. 8). One of the results of this was a dichotomy for blacks in America. Blacks living in the North were free and who, with restrictions, could advance themselves based on their own initiative and will. For instance, in the State of New York, slavery officially ended on July 4, 1827. While blacks in New York faced proscriptions for many years afterwards, which included travel restrictions and property ownership requirements in order to vote, they were able to partake of some types of economic and educational opportunities (Allen, 1968, p. 47).

Blacks living in the South were generally slaves who had no citizenship rights and no legal basis to improve or advance their interests. Although in some cities, such as Charleston, South Carolina, there were a significant number of educated or self-sufficient free blacks, most blacks in southern states were consistently denied any formal ways to improve their financial and intellectual capacities throughout the early to mid 1800s. In reference to the limited opportunities for slaves of the South to improve themselves intellectually during this time, historian James D. Anderson (1988) wrote that "during the three decades before the Civil War slaves lived in a society in which for them literacy was forbidden by law and symbolized as a skill that contradicted the status of slaves" (p. 16).

Even though labor was still a valuable commodity in America, half of the country had come to view slavery as detrimental to America's future. When referring to the division that existed in America in 1850 because of differing philosophies regarding the use of labor, Charles H. Wesley (1926) commented:

> Plantation economics and the domestic system were firmly established in the South while the industrial system had taken deep roots in the North and East. The North had found the free labor system profitable and supported it. In like manner the South was more determined than ever before to uphold a system of labor in which slavery was the fundamental condition . . . In all of their discussions, slave labor was regarded as a necessary condition of the economic system of the South. Controversies were raised frequently between northern and southern interests regarding the merits of the systems of labor which were carried on in these sections (p. 1).

Because of slavery, most blacks in the South were unable to make any economic progress, and only a small number of blacks improved themselves with regard to education prior to the end of the antebellum period. The blacks that did progress during this period were usually born free (Birnie, 1927, p. 13). Reportedly, free blacks received schooling well before the end of the antebellum period. However, many of the schools for free blacks were short lived, because of legislation that abruptly made them illegal (Vicary, 1999, p. 170). Following a conspiracy and slave revolt in the Charleston, South Carolina area led by Denmark Vesey, the South Carolina legislature passed a law in 1834 that prohibited the maintenance of schools by and for both free blacks and slaves (Holt, 1977, p. 53).

Some slaves were taught in underground schools by both free and enslaved blacks, who had been fortunate enough to have learned basic reading, writing and math. The underground schools were largely unsuccessful because the education of slaves had always been illegal and condemned by most white slave holders (Anderson, 1988, p. 16). Although underground schools later inspired blacks to pursue the creation of public educational institutions, education first became a reality with the assistance of the Union army and other northern relief organizations. With the aid of these organizations, a small number of southern blacks became literate (Taylor, 1924, p. 87).

During and after the antebellum period, southern blacks expressed a strong desire to improve their condition. Believing that through suffrage and education, they could become productive citizens, southern blacks organized and pushed for representation in electoral politics to achieve these rights. Receiving the right of suffrage, southern blacks voted in large numbers to elect delegates to state constitutional conventions. Their efforts led to an influx of blacks into elected positions in state government, which eventually resulted in significant constitutional gains for southern blacks during Reconstruction.

An important result of Reconstruction legislation was the constitutional right to public education. There were several southern states that included education in their constitutions and established public school systems. Among the first southern states to do so in 1868 were South Carolina, North Carolina, and Georgia (Du Bois, 1910, p. 798).

"South Carolina was unique among southern states in that it had no constitutional provision for education until Reconstruction and the adoption of a new constitution in 1868" (Vaughn, 1974, p. 51). The establishment of a system of education was made a primary objective at the 1868 Convention. With much debate, the Convention proposed and passed an educational provision that required all public schools, colleges and universities to be open to all children without distinction of race (Vaughn, 1974, p. 67).

While in South Carolina, the overwhelming majority of registered voters were black, white registered voters outnumbered blacks by a small margin in North Carolina. Furthermore, while the North Carolina Convention constitutionally provided that public schools would be established and open to children between the ages of 6 and 21 of North Carolina, it did not address the proposition of mixing the races in 1868 (Vaughn, 1974, p. 63).

Like North Carolina, Georgia also included a provision for public schools in 1868 without any mention of mixing blacks and whites. Jacqueline Jones (1980) concurred with Vaughn that public education developed slowly in Georgia. Jones indicated that an intense racial division within the Republican party and lack of funding were to blame. "Responsibility for the delay rested squarely on the shoulders of Republican state officials who, torn by political and personality difference remained distracted from the issue of education during their brief and stormy reign in the late 1860's" (Jones, 1980, p.

86). South Carolina's provision for education in 1868 differed from those in its neighboring states because it specifically and constitutionally provided the same rights to education for blacks and whites at the expense of the public.

Section one of this thesis discusses how education began in the South Carolina and includes an overview of the climate that existed as formal education began to take shape there. In section two, the focus moves to how the political organization of blacks led to their inclusion in electoral politics. Central to section two is the discussion of Randolph and his work in the state. Section three is a discussion of the 1868 Constitutional Convention and the educational provision, as well as barriers to education in spite of the constitutional law.

REVIEW OF THE LITERATURE

The findings of Alrutheus Ambush Taylor and W. E. B. Du Bois were central to this thesis. Both men were respected as formidable scholars and completed extensive research projects on the Reconstruction era. Their contributions were widely acknowledged and have informed later scholarship up until the present.

Mary White Ovington, a reviewer for the *Amsterdam News*, applauded Taylor's text, The Negro in South Carolina During the Reconstruction, in a 1925 article. She referred to Taylor as a careful scholar and described the text as needed to explain the Reconstruction in South Carolina (p. 16). In no way, however, did she interpret the text as incendiary or Taylor as being biased. In fact, Carter G. Woodson, in the book's preface, referred to Taylor's text as a disinterested account of black participation in South Carolina Reconstruction.

Taylor himself commented that his work was undertaken because he believed that previous accounts of the Reconstruction in South Carolina discredited blacks and their participation in politics. For Taylor, the political achievements of that period needed to be analyzed and interpreted holistically in order to demonstrate that blacks were major contributors during the period.

Black Reconstruction in America was also reviewed positively by some of its readers. For instance, the text was said to be full of facts and well researched by Rayford W. Logan, a reviewer for the *Journal of Negro History* in 1936. Logan even concluded that the work was the first attempt to interpret Reconstruction based on the economic principles of Karl Marx. Logan claimed that Du Bois' interpretation of the Reconstruction of America economically using a Marxist framework made the text unique and would command attention from other Reconstruction scholars. Around the same time that Logan reviewed the book, Jonathan Daniels, a member of the southern media, also commended Du Bois for his work. He thanked Du Bois for a noteworthy interpretation of Reconstruction as a conflict within the labor movement. Daniels asserted that Du Bois' interpretation was one that shed light on a freedom movement, not only for blacks, but for poor whites as well.[1]

Although there were many positive reviews of the text, there were also detractors from the text. *Time* magazine claimed that Du Bois was essentially trying to reconfigure Reconstruction history. Lewis (2000) recorded the following in reference to *Time* magazine's opinion of the Du Bois text:

> *Time* magazine's dismissal of Du Bois as an "ax-grinder" whose Reconstruction history was a "wonderland in which all familiar scenes and landmarks have been changed or swept away" hardly came as a surprise (p. 365).

Although the work was acknowledged as an outstanding text, it was also labeled as biased by reviewer Charles H. Wesley. Wesley referred to Du Bois' work as partisan propaganda. In a 1935 issue of the *Opportunity Journal*, Wesley wrote the following in reference to Du Bois: "It is almost impossible for one who takes a partisan view of a question to be honest with himself and frank with the facts" (p. 243). Nonetheless, the attention given to Black Reconstruction in America indicated that the text was an important and unique contribution to Reconstruction scholarship, the likes of which had not been seen before it.

---

[1] David Levering Lewis (2000) referred to Daniels as a contributing writer for the *Book of the Month Club News* (p. 365).

I believe that Du Bois served as an apologist, who was deliberate throughout his text in explaining his research findings on the efforts of blacks to gain citizenship rights while they faced powerful opposition. In doing so, he posited the notion that those who were against blacks and their participation in Reconstruction believed that blacks were naturally inferior. Furthermore, Du Bois was convinced that in South Carolina, a white oligarchy attempted to maintain political and economic power during the Reconstruction because it could not predict how the increase in the poor population, primarily because of the influx of blacks, would affect the status of the white landowners.

Although the Du Bois text was critical to the problem of this thesis, I attempted not to be partisan in composing this work. The Du Bois text was one of the most informative and comprehensive with regard to the role of blacks and Randolph during Reconstruction.

An important supporting text for this thesis was Joel Williamson's 1965 work, After Slavery: The Negro in South Carolina During Reconstruction, 1861-1877. In May of 1965, *The Library Journal* included only a minor assessment of the text. However, Williamson was credited for providing a revisionist approach of the activity of blacks in South Carolina during Reconstruction. Williamson's work was referred to as a noteworthy contribution to southern history overall, but was said to be "somewhat weakened by poorly substantiated generalizations" (Johnson, 1965, p. 2261).

In the winter of 1965, *The Virginia Quarterly Review* credited Williamson with shedding light on a period which had "until that time" remained dim. Williamson was commended for presenting significant but rare sources and being sensitive to the peculiarities of the time period. The following was written:

> Mr. Williamson has fitted his story together with unflinching honesty, but he keeps the score with sympathy and understanding. In showing the Negro as a conscious political agent, making choices, which were appropriate to his own best interest, the author dismisses one of the most tenacious stereotypes of the just post-slavery black man (p. 16).

The review also indicated that scholars would likely debate Williamson's contention that separation of the races was just as significant in South Carolina during early Reconstruction as it was at the end of the 19th century.

Thomas Holt's Black over White: Negro Political Leadership in South Carolina during Reconstruction was referred to as one of the best texts on South Carolina's black Republicans of its decade. In a review published in the June 1978 issue of the *American Historical Review*, Michael Perman claimed that the text stood apart from others similar to it because it did not simply tell who black legislators were, but it also described how black politicians functioned within the political system. Perman called attention to three "evaluative observations" that Holt made: (a) that black leaders operated independently of white supervision and control, (b) that both black and white Republican leaders failed to keep the party united, and (c) that there existed a division among black Republicans based on their complexion and status (slave or free), during the antebellum period (p. 812).

Leslie A. Schwalm's A Hard Fight For We: Women's Transition from Slavery to Freedom in South Carolina was the most recently published text evaluated for this study. A review of Schwalm's text appeared in the December 1998 issue of *The Journal of American History*. Reviewer Thavolia Glymph noted that Schwalm was a part of a trend to consider the importance of gender when interpreting slavery and freedom during the transition from the Civil War to Reconstruction. Schwalm analyzed the activity of slave women from the rice plantation districts of Low Country South Carolina and indicated that black women took a leading role in establishing families, rearing children and shaping early black freedom activity. While Glymph stated that Schwalm's emphasis on the importance of gender during the period was well proven, she also stated that Schwalm was unable to provide a convincing argument that gender "was at the center of slaves and freed people's efforts to construct their lives" (Glymph, 1998, p. 1083).

Because this project relied heavily on secondary sources, I deemed it important to consider the reactions of other readers to the major texts of this study. An analysis of available book reviews provided insight into how some readers of the texts, interpreted the works and the motives of the authors. Further, the book reviews prompted me to seek out primary sources for the purpose of confirming or disclaiming the assertions of an author.

METHOD

As the single participant in this historical research study, I began by reading materials that specifically discussed or included Benjamin Franklin Randolph. I initially found information that confirmed that Randolph was a prominent leader in South Carolina, but was one of many blacks that held leadership positions in the state during Reconstruction. Although I incorporated the fact that blacks held important leadership positions during Reconstruction into my thesis, I focused on Randolph and the period of time that he spent in South Carolina. There was consistent evidence that Randolph lived and worked in South Carolina from 1865 to 1868. Further investigation revealed additional documentation that referred to Randolph in Ohio and New York. The available information was used as either background information or supporting evidence for Randolph's work as a Chaplain and educator.

After deciding upon the time period, I investigated how Randolph and others contributed to the State of South Carolina during that time. Emphasis was placed on Randolph's efforts at the 1868 South Carolina Convention because Randolph began the discussion of an educational provision. However, I evaluated as much of Randolph's professional work in the state that I could find.

My investigation into Randolph and other black leaders was to find out how blacks were involved and to what extent blacks contributed to the progress of black citizenship rights during Reconstruction. An analysis of archival documents led to the discovery of invaluable primary source information. The documents were found at the

William R. Pullen and Robert W. Woodruff libraries in Atlanta, Georgia, as well as at the South Carolinian Historical Archives in Columbia, South Carolina.

As I anticipated, the extent to which blacks successfully contributed to the Reconstruction of South Carolina is debatable. However, it was clear at the conclusion of my research that blacks did actively participate during Reconstruction and that their participation was noteworthy in spite of racial hostility.

SECTION 1

THE EARLY EDUCATION OF BLACKS IN THE SOUTH

A complete picture of the early education of blacks in the South must include the activity of blacks before northern organizations entered the South. Although there was considerable debate as to exactly when and where learning first took place in the South, evidence suggested that blacks first began the learning process in the midst of slavery (Anderson, 1988, p. 6). Northern agencies encountered both slaves and some free blacks who had already begun to pursue literacy.

The early education of slaves in the South may be referred to as an underground movement because it first existed against the will and oblivious to slaveholders. The need for a covert plan to teach was because the education of slaves a dangerous proposition during slavery. As former slave William Henry Heard recalled: "We did not learn to read nor write, as it was against the law for any person to teach any slave to read: and any slave caught writing suffered the penalty of having his fore finger cut from his right hand, yet there were some who could read and write" (Anderson, 1988, p. 16). In spite of the dangers, Anderson suggested that a black school existed in Savannah, Georgia as early as 1833. Anderson stated that this school pre-dated but compared to one opened at Fortress Monroe, Virginia, under the leadership of black teacher Mary Peake. Current historiography referenced the Virginia school as one of the first schools operated

by slaves or free blacks in the South. Schools of this nature were called native schools by

John W. Alvord, who served as national Superintendent of schools for the Freedmen's Bureau. Alvord contended that native schools were common in virtually every southern state.[2] The two major characteristics of native schools were that they were run by free blacks or slaves, and they were self-sustaining. According to Anderson (1988) Alvord recorded the following in his Bureau reports:

> This educational movement among the freedmen has in it a self-sustaining element. This self-sustaining activity was rooted firmly in the slave experience and began to surface before the war's end (p. 7).

Native schools continued to evolve after the war ended. In fact, they became more prominent and even worked in conjunction with northern organizations such as the Freedmen's Bureau. The Freedmen's Bureau brought with it financial resources and qualified teachers to the South and its presence expanded the early education movement. However, native schools continued to maintain distinct identities characterized by black administrations. In some cases, native schools and Freedmen's Bureau schools existed together in venue but operated separately because many blacks preferred to send their children to schools controlled by blacks (Anderson, 1988, p. 7).

The Sabbath school was another type of school in which blacks demonstrated their ability and desire to be self-reliant with regard to education. Run by black churches, Sabbath schools first appeared near the end of the war and were different from native schools, primarily because instruction was provided on the weekends as opposed to during the week. This was invaluable to many blacks that could not attend school during the week because of work requirements. Although little was known about the Sabbath

---

[2] A detailed discussion of native schools and John W. Alvord appears in The Education of Blacks in the South, 1860-1935. While serving as national Superintendent of schools, Alvord traveled to most of the southern states and documented that native schools were common in each state that he visited (pp. 6-18).

school, Alvord recorded in Freedmen's Bureau reports that they were well attended and well run. In some areas of the South such as in North Carolina, Sabbath schools were reportedly more prevalent than native schools (Anderson, 1988, p. 12).

Both native and Sabbath schools served as evidence that black education began in the South largely because of the tireless efforts of blacks themselves. While northern organizations certainly influenced the direction of formal education, it was the grass-roots work of blacks that sustained schools throughout the South. In reference to this Anderson (1988) wrote,

> It was such local activities by ex-slaves that spurred the establishment of widespread elementary and literacy education and provided the grass roots foundation for the educational activities of northern missionary societies and the Freedmen's Bureau. To be sure, ex-slaves benefited greatly from the support of northern whites; but they were determined to achieve educational self-sufficiency in the long run with or without the aid of northerners. Their self-determination has escaped the attention of all but a few historians (p. 15).

Nonetheless, northern organizations became an integral part of formal education in South Carolina as they commenced to educate slaves displaced because of the Civil War.

<u>Northerners and the Movement to Educate Blacks in South Carolina</u>

Northerners entered the state of South Carolina in large numbers to engage in educational activity. According to Taylor (1924), northerners moved aggressively into the state before the Civil War ended. They responded to appeals from high-ranking individuals of the war such as General William Tecumseh Sherman who, along with other leaders of the Union army, observed that the overthrow of plantations left slaves needy and unorganized. Northern benevolent organizations and relief agencies believed that one way to assist the former slaves of South Carolina was to provide them with a basic education, and they began to do so as soon as they arrived.

Taylor contended that northern education systems were observed as early as 1861 in the state. They were first created and maintained by benevolent organizations and relief agencies such as the Boston Education Commission and the Pennsylvania Society when they moved into the state. These groups were among the first to come to the state, however, religious groups also came. Other organizations such as the Port Royal Relief Commission formed within the state.

The consensus, among the northerners involved in education, was that blacks needed to be literate. However, training in morality was also provided. Attention to the issues of literacy and morality were notable characteristics of the initial education efforts undertaken by northerners in South Carolina.

The Penn School, founded in 1862 by respected Philadelphia abolitionist Laura M. Towne, was an example of the early schools of instruction sponsored by northerners. Focusing on the population of blacks around the Sea Islands of South Carolina, the Penn School combined basic literacy and morality training. Of the Penn School, Taylor (1924) wrote,

> Its classes were grouped as primary, intermediate and higher, each conducted by a teacher in a separate room. The unvarying branches of study were reading, spelling, writing, geography and arithmetic (p. 83).

Although the Penn School, and others like it, achieved a measure of success, the impoverished condition of blacks and that of the state made it difficult for educators to create a stable educational system. Education workers arrived in a state that developed slowly due to racial division, poverty and opposition by landowners against blacks and their freedom from slavery. Thus education in South Carolina was an uncertain enterprise for the volunteers, organizations and societies that worked in the South, as well as blacks themselves. However, the influx of northern benevolent societies and relief agencies, religious groups, and eventually the Freedman's Bureau, began to formalize the structure for education. It is important to note that while Taylor (1924) did not emphasize the importance of the native and Sabbath schools in South Carolina, Anderson (1988) insisted that these schools were active and helped to sustain the early education movement throughout the South. This may be because Taylor focused on the Reconstruction period while Anderson presented more of a broad view of education over a longer period of time.

Both native and Sabbath schools could have been equally instrumental in preserving the movement, but Sabbath schools became more prevalent and grew directly in number with black churches. This was because blacks apparently withdrew from most white churches in the South after the Civil War (Du Bois, 1910, p. 781). But blacks did not abandon their faith, they simply moved to churches created and run by blacks. Informal congregations in which elder slave women (or spiritual mothers) "maintained their own religious services and practices away from the eye, and intervention, of whites", had existed in South Carolina's Low Country since the early 1800s (Schwalm, 1997, p. 70). The fact that blacks withdrew from white churches and had already adopted their own worship practices, may have led to the exponential growth in black Baptist and Methodist church membership. [3]

---

[3] Du Bois (1910) claimed that the African Methodist Episcopal church grew from 20,000 members in 1856

In addition to being places of emotional and spirited worship, black churches also served as important sites for instruction. Of the Sabbath schools, Anderson (1988) wrote the following:

> These Sunday schools were not devoted entirely to Bible study. As Booker T. Washington recalled from his own experience, "the principal book studied in the Sunday school was the spelling book" (p. 15).

Because of the black church, Sabbath schools were safe harbors for the education movement in South Carolina when the northern religious and benevolent organizations left.

The Freedmen's Bureau in South Carolina

The Freedmen's Bureau served many purposes in South Carolina, including providing teachers, managing the creation of schools and maintaining order. The latter function was how it differed most from the other benevolent organizations and relief agencies of the North. In addition, unlike the other organizations, the Freedmen's Bureau entered the South with federal support, after the Civil War had ended. It was understood that the Freedmen's Bureau served as a type of policing agency, which prompted Du Bois (1910) to write, "The Freedmen's Bureau was an attempt to establish a government guardianship over the blacks and insure their economic and civil rights" (p. 77). As a result, the Freedmen's Bureau was viewed with disdain and was unwelcome by most southern whites. This was the case, even though the organization had done little to combat the invidious environment that existed outside of its schools because of racial hostility. Nonetheless, this temporary agency was instrumental in preserving stability

---

to 75,000 in 1866. The black Baptist churches, he stated, grew from 150,000 in 1850 to 500,000 by 1870 (p. 782).

and expanding educational opportunities in South Carolina before also withdrawing from the state.

Barriers that Affected the Development of South Carolina

Two major barriers affected the development of South Carolina that no outside organization was able to prevent. The first was a perennial racial division. The white landowners believed that blacks were their property and this sentiment did not immediately change. Even whites that did not own significant amounts of land were protective of the positions that they held in the state because of slavery. However, many blacks apparently disagreed with the notion that blacks should continue to be subservient and that blacks were naturally inferior to whites. The presence of northerners living and working in the state, had very little affect on how whites viewed blacks, and whites were not deterred from being hostile towards northerners or blacks (Taylor, 1924, p.19). Emancipation and the end of the Civil War actually created more open hostility as whites resisted the changes that were taking place in their state. Slavery remained the guiding principle by which most whites, rich and poor, viewed the role of blacks. In explanation, Taylor (1924) wrote,

> The emancipation of the slaves was submitted only in so far as chattel slavery in the old form could not be continued. But, although the freedman was no longer considered the property of the individual master, he was considered the slave of society. The whites had much difficulty in abandoning the idea that the blacks were property by natural right (p. 21).

The perceived role of blacks by whites in post-Civil War South Carolina became more evident with the establishment of the state's black code. The code was designed to restore white domination in race and labor relations. In addition to forcing the newly free blacks to assume stringent labor roles, the code also restricted free and slave-born blacks to only menial tasks. The code also established severe reprisals for violating labor contracts (Schwalm, 1997, p. 181).

A second barrier that affected the development of South Carolina was the impoverished condition of the state after the war. The state had been ravaged and many of the institutions and businesses in the state were severely impaired or destroyed. South Carolina had derived the majority of its tax revenue from assessments on the goods and services that merchants, bankers and other businesses provided. These businesses became unable to provide tax revenue to the state (Du Bois, 1935, p. 401).

Real estate had also decreased in value. In fact, Du Bois contended that real estate in South Carolina was valued at nearly 60 percent less than it had been (Du Bois, 1935, p. 401). Other assets, such as stocks and endowments, lost much of their value. The question of how to best meet the financial needs of the state was left for the incoming Reconstruction government to address. They would eventually decide to increase tax assessments on land, which placed a heavy burden on the landowners (Williamson, 1965, p. 148).

The new system of taxation that the state government had decided upon was bitterly opposed by the landowners. Since landowners believed that their property was the key to their former power, they would not support the higher tax on land. Landowners felt that the tax would make it difficult for them to hold on to their land and to maintain their significant position in society as landowners. Landowners opposed the new system of taxation, mainly by non-compliance with tax assessments (Williamson, 1965, p. 158).

Although the Reconstruction government proposed to use taxation funds to assist in the refurbishment of the state's infrastructure and the development of a new and more public state, many landowners believed that the predominately black Reconstruction government was misguided and would waste money or create unnecessary services for blacks. Du Bois, theorized that the landed aristocracy had governed South Carolina informally until the Reconstruction era and maintained a notable amount of influence during Reconstruction because of the relationships that they had developed for decades. If this theory is true, then the landed aristocracy can be referred to as an oligarchy. Du Bois (1935) wrote "they made the functions of the state just as few as possible, and did by private law and on private plantations most the things, which in other states were carried on by the local and state governments" (p. 408).

Du Bois suggested that the oligarchy was deliberate in opposing the Reconstruction government because it was predominately black and that the oligarchy used bribery to sway poor residents as well as legislators.[4] Du Bois also suggested that the oligarchy contributed to the slander that complicated the state government's efforts to secure lines of credit from outside the state.[5] Evidence suggests that Democratic

---

[4] Du Bois (1935) theorized that bribery was effective because most black and white residents of South Carolina were poverty-stricken at the time. He indicated that even governmental officials consistently accepted bribes in spite of holding important leadership positions. Many of the state's governmental officials were also poor. Du Bois implied that bribery may have afforded the oligarchy a significant amount of internal political control (p. 409).

[5] Du Bois (1935) recorded an incident involving Governor James L. Orr. Orr visited New York City for the purpose of borrowing money on the credit of South Carolina. Orr stated "I called at several of the most prominent banking houses to effect the negotiation of the required loan, and they refused to advance any money upon our state securities, for those securities had already been branded with the threat of a speedy repudiation by the political opponents of the administration, who have ever since howled the same cry against the credit of the state (p. 410).

legislators may have slandered the Republican dominated Reconstruction government until the Democrats gained majority power.[6] Government officials were able to raise a limited amount of funds from outside of the state, but at substantially higher than normal interest rates. The high interest rates were based on the perception by other states that the credit of South Carolina was poor.

The former landed aristocracy had embraced and lived in affluence because of the land they owned and slave labor. Thus resentment over the proposition of finding ways to support the cultivation and harvest of crops in the absence of slavery, and fulfilling other physical needs to maintain their land, may have also contributed to why an oligarchy opposed blacks in the legislature. In essence, Reconstruction was a revolution to the former landed aristocracy because it no longer owned the rights to the vast black labor pool. Furthermore, the Reconstruction government began to enact laws that gave rights to this new class of citizens. By 1868, blacks began to make significant progress. They had gained voting rights and political power, which allowed them to legally achieve citizenship rights. Education was one area that blacks continued to view as most important to their progress as citizens. Consequently, blacks quickly pursued the rights to a formal system of public education.

The First Petition for a State System of Education

The first formal petition for a state system of education to be added to South Carolina's Constitution occurred on March 3, 1868 at the Constitutional Convention. Randolph was the first state official to initiate the discussion of an educational provision, which materialized into an education article at the Convention (Taylor, 1924, p. 134).

---

[6] F.L. Cardozo stated this in an interview appearing in the June 22, 1874 issue of the *New York Times* (p. 5).

Randolph was a Senator representing Orangeburg, South Carolina, at the Convention and had served earlier in the state as Union Army Chaplain, missionary and administrator. He worked first with the Freedmen's Bureau as an educator before becoming involved in electoral politics (Williamson, 1965, p. 220). However, Randolph was only one of a large contingent of black leaders who migrated South during Reconstruction. Carter G. Woodson (1918) theorized that this migration of black leaders continued well into the 1870s.

Randolph was a leader among black Republicans in South Carolina, a successful organizer of people and a fearless advocate of equality (Williamson, 1965, p. 365). Randolph's political skills, passion for equality, and a commitment to education led to his petition at the 1868 Convention.

SECTION 2

RANDOLPH AND BLACK CITIZENSHIP

Benjamin Franklin Randolph

Randolph was born in Kentucky circa 1837. Historian Daniel W. Hamilton (1999) indicated that the names of his parents are unknown, but Randolph was born free to a white father and black mother (p. 121). As a child, Randolph was educated in Ohio, and entered the preparatory school of Oberlin College in 1854. He remained in the preparatory school until 1857 before entering Oberlin's collegiate department. While in college, Randolph studied liberal arts and theology at Oberlin's seminary. However, Randolph did not graduate from either Oberlin's collegiate department or seminary. Williamson (1965) contended that Randolph entered the ordination process of the Methodist Episcopal Church between 1862 and 1864. Where Randolph began the process is unknown.

A letter written by Randolph to a Buffalo, New York newspaper on January 28, 1863, connected him to the Vine Street African Methodist Episcopal (A.M.E.) church. Randolph's letter discussed an Emancipation Celebration, which was held at the church in reference to the signing of the Emancipation Proclamation by President Lincoln.[7]

Randolph described a celebratory religious service that began at 10:00 a.m. and lasted until 2:00 p.m. In fact, Randolph recorded that Deaton Dorrell an elder in the A.M.E. church, delivered a sermon entitled, "How shall we celebrate this day?" Dorrell was a prominent member of the New York Conference of the A.M.E. church for more than 30 years.[8]

---

[7] This letter appears in detail as an editorial entitled "Emancipation Celebration at Buffalo, N.Y." in the February 14, 1863 edition of the *Black Abolitionist Papers*.
[8] A picture of Deaton Dorrell can also be found in Alexander W. Wayman, *Cyclopedia of African Methodism* (Baltimore: Methodist Book Depository, 1882) 53, 117.

The service was also diverse. Both blacks and whites attended this four-hour celebration. The presence of whites at this service confirmed that there existed a strong anti-slavery sentiment in the North.

At 8:00 p.m., congregants gathered once more at the church for what Randolph referred to as a mass meeting. After a prayer by Elder Dorrell and a song, Randolph delivered the proclamation. He wrote that it was well received by the congregants who were then addressed by the evening speaker. In closing his letter, Randolph wrote that remarks were given and that the attendees ate supper before leaving.

Randolph's participation at the Buffalo Emancipation Celebration confirmed that he was politically active and associated with black religious leaders prior to his work in South Carolina. Furthermore, Randolph's participation as speaker and the fact that he held the title of Chief Scribe of the Day, indicated that he was respected as a speaker and a writer.

It is unclear how long Randolph remained in the State of New York or if he lived and worked elsewhere prior to his migration to South Carolina. However, before Randolph entered South Carolina, blacks had already responded to their emancipation from slavery. They were beginning to organize themselves, as evidenced by their participation in the National Union Convention, to seek the rights that would be afforded to them as free citizens.

Black Political Organization in South Carolina during Reconstruction

Du Bois (1935) theorized that blacks earnestly desired to be acknowledged as citizens and that their push for citizenship could be connected to their initial efforts to organize themselves politically. Their earliest success at political organization occurred in 1864 at Port Royal. In 1864, blacks elected representative delegates to attend the National Union Convention. The National Union Convention was a convention controlled by whites who supported the Union and Vice President Andrew Johnson. Johnson succeeded Abraham Lincoln to become President of the United States after Lincoln was assassinated on April 14, 1865 (Rousseve, 1937, p. 101). The Convention proclaimed the following: (a) that a state could not secede or exclude any other state from the union, (b) that each state had the constitutional right to decide for itself the qualifications for voting, within its borders, (c) that the constitution could not be legally amended except with all the states voting in Congress and action by all the legislatures, and (d) that southern states should not restore slavery (Du Bois, 1935, p. 389).

Accordingly, the black delegates were dissatisfied with the National Union Convention, because there was no endorsement of universal suffrage. In addition, blacks may have also been disappointed because the Convention was marked by the presence of many well known Democrats, and few Republicans (Du Bois, 1935, p. 315). Since Taylor (1924), theorized that most black leaders were attracted to the Republican Party, the black delegates at this Convention could have been disheartened by the lack of a strong Republican presence. Although Randolph quickly became an advocate for the Republican Party while in South Carolina, he first entered the state as a military Chaplain.

Randolph as Union Army Chaplain

By an appointment of the Union Army, Randolph served as a Chaplain for the Twenty-Sixth Colored Infantry. He was one of fourteen black men to receive such an appointment. A two-page report from Randolph, dated May 31, 1865, was composed from his post in Beaufort, South Carolina.

This report from Chaplain Randolph to a Brigadier General Thomas is revealing about his work as a Chaplain. It indicated that the moral and religious condition of black soldiers was of the utmost importance. Randolph also indicated that religious meetings were well received and that there was great interest in them. He acknowledged that a teacher from the American Missionary Association was either assisting or directing the regimental school. Regimental schools were set up at Union Army installations to deal primarily with the large influx of illiterate blacks into the Union Army. Interestingly, Randolph concluded that the moral condition of the soldiers was above average. However, he noted that white commissioned officers threatened to subvert this by being profane and setting poor examples. Randolph's comments follow in an excerpt from the report (Berlin, 1982, Records of the Adjutant General's office, group 94):

> Religious meetings are frequent and tolerable well. Many manifest an interest in meetings. The regimental School is taught by a teacher furnished by American Missionary Association. Many of the men manifest much interest in learning, and great good is being done in this respect, and many of these men will return to their homes better Scholars, and better morally. The greatest ostensible evil in this regiment is, profanity. Some of the white Com. Officers persist in this evil habit, which makes it very difficult for the Chaplain to check it on the part of the men. The poor oppressed negro of this land needs the most wholesome example set before him to elevate him, but this is one bad example, set by those whom he

looks up to for example, and which confirms him in his degredation [sic]. Would that for humanity's sake it could be stoped! [sic] (p. 142).

From Randolph's report it was clear that the soldiers' progress in religion and education was essential to the Chaplain's assessment of the regiment. A moral dimension can be seen as well, since Randolph discussed stealing, gambling and other delinquencies. The importance of education can be drawn from the fact that a large number of soldiers were learning to read and write during the month of May. Nearly twenty-five percent of the regiment was participating in the education program. From this report, it appeared that Randolph deemed it important to discuss morality and education. The level of the Chaplain's theological convictions is not relayed.

Randolph and the American Missionary Association

Randolph's reference to the American Missionary Association (AMA), in his Chaplain's report, was revealing for two reasons. First, since Hamilton (1999), contended that Randolph served in South Carolina with the AMA in 1865, as a post-Civil War missionary, Randolph's report indicated that he became associated with the AMA while he served as Union Army Chaplain. This may explain why Randolph returned to the state. Second, the reference was indicative of his knowledge that the AMA needed qualified teachers in their efforts to assist blacks. Thomas C. Holt (1977), wrote the following about the AMA:

> The most influential and best-financed northern society in South Carolina was the American Missionary Association, which had been established in 1846 as an anti-slavery organization (p. 81).

Robert C. Morris, author of <u>Reading, Riting, and Reconstruction</u> (1973), referred to the AMA as an abolitionist movement that was strictly evangelical "fashioning a program which combined Christian anti-slavery activity with evangelism" (p. 311). With limited educational work in Indiana, Ohio and Kentucky, the AMA sought teachers who embraced a level of religiosity to perform missionary work. Morris (1973) further wrote "the AMA placed 'missionary spirit' at the top of its list of teacher qualifications. No one need apply who was not 'prepared to endure hardness as a soldier of Jesus Christ' (p. 67). One might then conclude, that the AMA and societies like it embraced a pedagogical conception that was fundamentally religious. Furthermore, the reference to a combined Christian anti-slavery activity and evangelism means that AMA teachers may have been focused on spreading a Christian message; thus, they were first and foremost evangelists, and second, teachers. Randolph's reference to this organization in his Chaplain's report and his connection with them as a missionary, imply that he was influenced philosophically by this organization. It might also be concluded that Randolph's desire to work in South Carolina was heavily influenced by his personal religious convictions, which likely gained him acceptance into the AMA.

Randolph began his service in South Carolina at a pivotal time of independent political organization by the black population. By the fall of 1865, Randolph had become a surrogate leader in South Carolina because of his work with the Union Army and the AMA. One indication that Randolph was politically active in the state, was his involvement at the Colored People's Convention of South Carolina.

<u>The Colored People's Convention of South Carolina</u>

Given the failure of the National Union Convention to directly address the concerns of blacks, blacks organized the Colored People's Convention of South Carolina. This further indicated that they were determined to organize politically. The Colored People's Convention of South Carolina was held at Zion Church of Charleston, South Carolina in November of 1865. This Convention lasted six days and included 51 delegates (Foner & Walker, 1989, Minutes, p. 286). Although he was not a delegate, Randolph was invited to participate in this Convention. He delivered a speech in response to an open call to the audience by the Convention President (Foner & Walker, 1980, Minutes, pp. 288-301).

The idea of advancing the interest of blacks was a recurring one throughout this Convention. For instance, on the first day of the Convention, the following was recorded:

> A Convention of the colored people of the State of South Carolina, will assemble in the city of Charleston, on the third Monday of November, instant, being the twentieth day of the month, for the purpose of deliberating upon the plans best calculated to advance the interest of our people, to devise means for our mutual protection, and to encourage the industrial interest of the State (Foner & Walker, 1980, Minutes, p. 288).

On the second day, the delegates specifically discussed education as a means of self-improvement. The delegates submitted the following resolution, revealing the importance of education:

> Whereas, "Knowledge is power" And an educated and intelligent people can neither be held in, nor reduced to slavery; we will insist upon the establishment of

> good schools for the thorough education of our children throughout the State…we solemnly urge the parents and guardians of the young to see that schools are at once established in every neighborhood and when so established, to see to it that every child of proper age, is kept in regular attendance upon the same (Foner & Walker, 1980, Minutes, p. 290).

The fact that education was discussed early during the Convention, suggested that it was of the utmost importance. In addition, the prominence of education at this Convention indicated that Randolph might have simply voiced a sentiment that already existed among blacks, when he began the education discussion three years later at the Constitutional Convention.

The third, fourth and fifth days of the Convention were devoted to considering various resolutions submitted by the Business Committee and discussions on the proper conduct of blacks. On November 24, 1865, the sixth and final day of the Convention, the delegates recorded an "Address: Of the Colored State Convention To the People of the State of South Carolina" (Foner & Walker, 1980, Minutes, p. 298). In this address, the Convention proclaimed their belief that all men, regardless of race, were created equally. They also asked for equitable treatment for blacks. An excerpt reads:

> We simply desire that we shall be recognized as men; that we have no obstructions placed in our way; that the same laws which govern white men shall direct colored men; that we have the right of trial by a jury of our peers, that schools be opened or established for our children; that we be permitted to acquire homesteads for ourselves and children; that we be dealt with as others, in equity and justice (Foner & Walker, 1980, Minutes, p. 300).

The Colored People's Convention was civil and focused. It confirmed that blacks wanted their interests and needs to be respected. They were forthright in delivering this message to South Carolina and to America.

After 1865, the AMA, Freedmen's Bureau and other organizations were instrumental in the establishment of schools in the Charleston area and other parts of the state. Taylor (1924) noted that this was because most of the hostility associated with the war had ceased by this time (p. 85).

In addition to assisting with the founding of such schools as the Avery Normal Institute in Charleston, the AMA was an important point of departure for Randolph. After serving with the AMA until 1866, Randolph co-founded a newspaper called the *Charleston Journal* with Congregationalist minister Ennals J. Adams; he subsequently commenced his professional work as an educator and increased his political activism (Garraty, 1999, p. 21).

Randolph and Equality

In 1867, Randolph joined the Freedmen's Bureau and was appointed an agent of the education division. He served first as a teacher and later as Assistant Superintendent of schools for the Bureau in South Carolina. While serving as the Bureau's Assistant Superintendent, Randolph proved to be an outspoken advocate for equality among the races (Hamilton, 1999, p. 121).

Already politically involved by this time, Randolph the educator and Republican, made a statement for equality at the second Republican State Convention held in July of 1867. Because he was a participant at the Colored People's Convention two years earlier, Randolph must have known that the consensus among the black Republicans was that blacks voters wanted fairness in matters of human rights. When allowed to speak, he declared:

> We are laying the foundation of a new structure here, and the time has come when we shall have to meet things squarely, and we must meet them now or never. The day is coming when we must decide whether the two races shall live together or not (Williamson, 1965, p. 220).

Randolph was considerably more aggressive in expressing racial equality than the Colored People's Convention was in its proclamations. The statement read as if Randolph was outspoken and a visionary. He openly expressed an interest in seeing equality among whites and blacks as quickly as possible. However, it is unclear why Randolph was this direct about equality so soon after emancipation and while a strong racial division existed in the state. Williamson (1965) wrote that observers interpreted Randolph's statement as an attempt to require white and black children to attend schools together (p. 220).

Also in 1867, Randolph became the vice president of the Republican State executive committee. Randolph was active and furthered the recruiting efforts of the Republican Party by canvassing the State to find persons willing to join the party (Williamson, 1965, p. 366). He eventually became the party's Chairman. Many white Republicans denounced Randolph's election to the position of Chairman. Although these white Republicans had welcomed blacks into the party, they were not confident that blacks could successfully hold leadership positions. In reference to Randolph's election, Holt (1977) wrote the following:

When Randolph was elected, several conservative Republicans were reported to have staged a walkout, and plans were laid to undo his authority (p. 105). Although feuding existed internally, the Republican Party wielded a high level of influence among blacks in South Carolina around this time. Blacks were attracted to the party because it promoted reform and had expressed interest in issues such as education and suffrage (Taylor, 1924, p. 197).

Blacks and Citizenship Rights

Although black Republicans were active and influential in South Carolina, Du Bois contended that white military commanders and northern capitalists first assisted blacks with their efforts to gain citizenship rights. For instance, in March of 1867, General Edward Canby ordered blacks to serve on juries. This was significant because it promoted black participation in the governing process. As for northern capitalists, they implicitly encouraged black involvement in the economy because of eagerness to promote their self-interest involving trade and enterprise in the state (Du Bois, 1935, p. 387).

By the fall, the United States Congress had enacted the Reconstruction laws of 1867. The Reconstruction laws required former seceded southern states to do the following: (a) frame a new constitution decided upon by voters without distinction of race or color, in order to be represented in Congress, (b) have the constitution approved by the majority of voters and by Congress, (c) adopt the 14th Amendment to the United States Constitution (Rousseve, 1937, p. 102). "The 14th Amendment, adopted in 1866, declared in part that blacks were citizens of the United States and of the states wherein they might live, that the citizenship rights of freedmen might not be abridged by any state and that all citizens were entitled to equal protection of the laws" (Rousseve, 1937, p. 103).

The Reconstruction laws of 1867 allowed 80,500 black men to vote in South Carolina, nearly twice the number of whites. These new black voters elected black leaders to represent them the following year at the 1868 Convention. Twenty-one of 31 counties had black majorities and black leadership emerged as the voice of the black populace (Du Bois, 1935, p. 388).

A primary concern for many whites was whether men who had previously held slave status were prepared to properly exercise this right of citizenship. Former slave and Reconstruction legislator Beverly Nash responded (Du Bois, 1935):

> I believe, my friends and fellow citizens, we are not prepared for this suffrage. But we can learn. Give a man tools and let him commence to use them, and in time he will learn a trade. So it is with voting. We may not understand it at the start, but in time we shall learn to do our duty... (p. 391).

Nash believed that blacks were just as capable of voting properly as poor whites had done in South Carolina for many years. He was in favor of universal suffrage without regard to property or education.[9]

A secondary concern for whites was the direction South Carolina would move in with the influence of black voting. The enactment of the Reconstruction laws and the overwhelming response to them by blacks alarmed some whites. Apparently, it was not anticipated that blacks would be in a position to participate this quickly in political affairs.

---

[9] Nash shared his views with a correspondent for the *New York Times* on March 16, 1867. He was attending a meeting of freedmen in Columbia, to celebrate the Reconstruction suffrage bill.

The Reaction to Black Citizenship

The Reconstruction laws of 1867 essentially made black voters citizens of South Carolina. However, black citizenship was either accepted or rejected by whites. Governor James L. Orr, who served South Carolina from 1865 to 1868, and a group of his supporters, accepted the black participation in Reconstruction and decided to work with this changed circumstance. However, Confederate General Wade Hampton, who owned large plantations in South Carolina and Mississippi, was less straightforward in his position. Hampton led an informal group of his supporters that rejected the black citizenship idea but devised a plan to control the black vote by appearing to accept the Reconstruction laws. A third group was led by former Governor Benjamin F. Perry. Perry had served as acting Governor of South Carolina in 1865. He was appointed to this position by President Andrew Johnson. This group also rejected the black citizenship idea and decided to register as many whites as possible to vote against a Constitutional Convention (Du Bois, 1935, p. 389). The group met just a week prior to the Constitutional Convention, and drafted the following statement:

> Blacks are utterly unfitted to exercise the highest function of a citizen...We protest against this subversion of the social order, whereby an ignorant and depraved race is placed in power and influence above the virtuous, the educated, and the refined (Du Bois, 1935, p. 389).

Nevertheless, the South Carolina Constitutional Convention took place with black delegates holding 70 out of 124 positions (Holt, 1977, p. 35). This constituted an eight-vote majority for the blacks. The local media reported that the black delegates were orderly and well behaved throughout the Convention (Du Bois, 1935, p. 404).

Although the question of whether blacks were prepared to handle citizenship apparently dominated the minds of whites, an equally important question was, "Could a majority black legislature effectively govern?" (Du Bois, 1935, p. 387). Du Bois noted that as many as fifty of the black legislators were former slaves. The concern over black governance in 1868 was probably even more immediately pertinent to whites than was black suffrage. Whites generally believed that blacks were inferior human beings who lacked the ability to make effective leadership decisions. However, Du Bois (1935) theorized that blacks did not have as much decision-making power as was widely believed because white legislators held direct power. To Du Bois, it was questionable whether black legislators exercised true autonomy in their decision-making. Interestingly, Holt (1977) made the following comment about Du Bois' perspective on blacks and the power that they held in state government:

> Du Bois, for example, accepted the idea of the essential powerlessness of blacks in South Carolina's Reconstruction government in order to minimize the culpability of blacks for the corruption of that government, even though the acceptance of the former idea actually contradicts his thesis of black labor's control of the government (p. 99).

Du Bois also believed that corruption was a problem in the legislature, in part, because of the general misconception that black legislators needed to be cajoled or persuaded, and also because an oligarchy bribed government officials in South Carolina. The group did not agree with black participation in government or electoral politics and was determined to preserve power (Du Bois, 1935, p. 387).

Corruption during Reconstruction

One of the largest acts of corruption in South Carolina during Reconstruction was initiated by external forces. It involved the misuse of railroad funding. Beginning just prior to 1850, the railroad increased significantly in the decade that followed. It grew from 289 to 973 miles. However, within the next five years, railroad mileage increased nominally to only 1,007 because of the Civil War (Du Bois, 1935, p. 393). Du Bois asserted that it was wise for the Reconstruction legislature of South Carolina to embrace railroad expansion when they gained power. The railroad was important for the State to have an opportunity to grow and to prosper. To fund the railroad expansion, the Reconstruction legislature allowed the issuance of bonds on the credit of the state. This was a standard procedure. However, businessmen who were dishonest defrauded the state. Du Bois (1935) wrote the following in reference to this fraudulent activity:

> The difficulty was that a flock of cormorants whose business was cheating and manipulation in the issue and sale of bonds and other certificates of enterprise, moved first West and then South, and took charge of railroad promotion. They were largely Northern financiers, in some cases already discredited in the centers of finance and driven out of the overworked investment fields North and West. They came south with an address and a technique, which only trained, experience, and honest administrators could have withstood. They flaunted the chances of quick and easy money before the faces of ruined planters, small Northern investors, and the few Negroes who had some little capital. The result was widespread graft, debt and corruption in South Carolina, North Carolina, Florida, Georgia, Louisiana, and in other states (p. 407).

The end result was a railroad system that had not grown and was poor in quality compared to other states. The state was also in debt because of the railroad and the State's bonds were insufficient to cover the debt. Du Bois (1935) indicated that black legislators were accused of the troubles associated with the railroad.

Williamson (1965) concurred that persons from outside of South Carolina initiated corruption of the railroad system. He stated that a "Railroad Ring" developed which may have included governmental officials (p. 384). However, Williamson did not make a connection between railroad fraud and the perception that black legislators were responsible for the problems associated with the railroad.

Throughout the South, it was believed that dishonesty involving public officials had been a problem even before Reconstruction. Clerks, sheriffs and even Treasury officials defrauded state governments regularly (Du Bois, 1910, p. 790). Although Du Bois did not deny that blacks of the Reconstruction legislature were also part of the corruption in South Carolina, he vehemently opposed the idea that blacks were solely responsible for corruption. Quite simply, Du Bois and even Taylor believed that blacks in government had no direct control over those committees that made financial decisions or dispersed money. Blacks received and used illicit gifts, but did not have the power to generate them. Author David Levering Lewis (2000) commented,

> Corruption in the post-Civil War South was color-blind and no respecter [sic] of partisan affiliation, with carpetbaggers and redeemers evenly matched in the potlatch of state contracts and railroad bonds. Furthermore, as Taylor documented, Negro legislators never controlled the key committees for graft, not even in South Carolina where they held a majority in the lower house (p. 367).

To Lewis, blacks may have been accused of being extravagant, dishonest and of being incompetent as officials; however, Reconstruction was an era of extravagance in which all legislators were direct or unwitting participants.

Du Bois contended that the accusations against the black legislators were in some cases completely fabricated and in most cases highly exaggerated. Du Bois (1910) wrote,

> The chief charges against the black governments are extravagance, theft, and incompetence of officials. There is no serious charge that these governments threatened civilization or the foundations of social order. The charge is that they threatened property, and that they were inefficient. These charges are in part undoubtedly true, but they are often exaggerated. . . In fact, the extravagance, although great, was not universal, and much of it was due to the extravagant spirit pervading the whole country in a day of inflated currency and speculation. The ignorance was deplorable but a deliberate legacy from the past, and some of the extravagance and much of the effort was to remedy this ignorance. The incompetence was in part real and in part emphasized by the attitude of the whites of the better class (p. 789).

The racial division in South Carolina grew wider during Reconstruction as blacks were portrayed as incompetent thieves. This idea may have only been partially true, but it was pervasive. Poor whites quickly accepted it and resented both black legislators and the new black citizens (Taylor, 1924, p. 300).

Structural Change in South Carolina

In South Carolina, race was the major issue that divided whites and blacks during Reconstruction. However, if race were completely removed from the state in 1868, a fundamental difference in the structure of South Carolina would have still existed than prior to Reconstruction. This was because South Carolina's poor population became more significant both numerically and economically, with the addition of the former black slaves who were set free. Prior to the war, the owners of land and slaves became wealthy, having both the land and labor to produce goods for the exchange of capital. For this reason the term "landed aristocracy" is often used to refer to this group. After the war, this landed aristocracy lost one hundred percent of the pre-war value in slaves and from fifty to one hundred percent in land. Some of these wealthy whites lost everything (Du Bois, 1935, p. 384). The remaining white property holders were faced with a new economy in which the new and enlarged labor pool could potentially make more demands as free laborers and possess some of their land. There was a considerable amount of doubt expressed by whites as to whether the former slave could make a smooth transition into the role of free laborer (Williamson, 1965, p. 70). Meanwhile, former slaves in most cases eagerly moved away from former labor relationships and embraced freedom.

Blacks and Freedom

One way in which blacks gave evidence of their desire to be free during Reconstruction was with the enthusiasm in which they embraced education. Anderson (1988) noted that Booker T. Washington observed:

> Few people who were not right in the midst of the scenes can form any exact idea of the intense desire, which the people of my race showed for education. It was a whole race trying to go to school. Few were too young, and none too old, to make the attempt to learn (p. 5).

The reference to education as a means of self-improvement at the Colored People's Convention of South Carolina confirmed that former slaves likely viewed education as either a tool for securing what they wanted, or the one asset that could not be taken away. Importantly, blacks appeared to understand that their freedom meant they could use their labor power to benefit them educationally. Alvord recorded the following in his Freedmen's Bureau reports:

> More than one instance could be already given where a school in the interior has been started from this motive... The head of one of the largest of the timber and turpentine enterprises in South Carolina told me that he formerly had hired only men, but he had now learned that he must have families too, and that this could only be done by allowing them patches of land, treating them properly, paying them well and giving them schools (Anderson, 1988, p. 21).

Another way in which blacks exhibited the desire to be free at this time was by the swiftness that blacks withdrew from predominantly white religious institutions to establish their own separate religious institutions. Although as early as the 1830s, the white Baptist organizations evangelized blacks in large numbers, blacks never controlled how congregations formed. In reference to this Schwalm (1997) wrote that "southern planters attempted to Christianize their slaves and manipulate their membership in the church as a form of social control" (p. 70).

Williamson (1965) concluded that the primary objective of white Baptists prior to the Reconstruction era was to reconcile blacks to the condition of slavery.

The religious organizations of the North first assisted blacks of the South in the development of their own religious organizations. The more influential organizations were missionaries and Methodists of the North. Black religious organizations grew more rapidly during Reconstruction than they had immediately following the war. The A.M.E. church, which was controlled by blacks and had been formally established in Philadelphia by 1816, was one of the leading religious organizations. Writing on this topic, Williamson (1965) observed:

> At the end of Reconstruction, about one hundred thousand blacks in South Carolina belonged to churches inaugurated by out-of-state missionaries. Probably slightly more than this number belonged to churches, which had been established by the self-inspired secession of Negro members from churches dominated by Southern whites (p. 195).

The importance of education and religion to blacks may be supported by the fact that 76 percent of the black political leaders in 1868 were either teachers or ministers by profession (Holt, 1977, p. 38).

Being both a teacher and minister, Randolph clearly involved himself with the issues of equality and education in South Carolina. He appeared to view these issues as central to black citizenship and freedom. Although Randolph was not the only black leader to promote equality or public education, few others were as outspoken as Randolph. However, it was the collective effort of black leaders that contributed to the establishment of the constitutional right to education.

Ω

SECTION 3

THE DEVELOPMENT OF A PUBLIC SYSTEM OF EDUCATION

The end of the Civil War brought with it the requirement that the former Confederate states reconstitute themselves as a condition for readmittance into the Union. All of the states did this successfully during Reconstruction with black voters and elected officials participating in the process. Public education became a notable component of the constitutions of the former Confederate states during this rebuilding process. However, not all of the southern states specifically included in their educational provisions that schools should be open to both races during the Reconstruction era. The South Carolina Constitutional Convention though, clearly authorized an educational provision in 1868 that opened schools to whites and blacks (Vaughn, 1974, pp. 51- 77).

The 1868 Constitutional Convention

It was as a senator that Randolph participated in the South Carolina Constitutional Convention of 1868, which began on January 14 and was held in Charleston. The

Convention was noteworthy because blacks served as legislators in South Carolina for the first time in the history of the state and also because it was the first Constitutional Convention in America in which blacks constituted the majority of a State House of Representatives. Because of the political power of blacks, it was also "the first experiment in this country of working out a government based on the cooperation of the two races" (Taylor, 1924, p. 127). Furthermore, since blacks outnumbered whites in the state legislature, the short-term destiny of South Carolina was in the hands of the black delegates as representatives of the black population, which had voted them into office.

Randolph took the liberty of addressing the delegates at the Constitutional Convention immediately after the "creation of a state commission for buying lands and selling them to the freedmen" (Du Bois, 1935, p. 395). On March 3, the 41st session of the Convention, Randolph gave his perspective on race and equality. He asserted that slavery was an institution that the forefathers of America felt would eventually end, and that it was time for blacks to receive equal treatment and protection from the law. The following is an excerpt of the address:

> Our forefathers were no doubt anti-slavery men, and they intended that slavery should die out. Consequently, the word color is not to be found in the Constitution or Declaration of Independence. On the contrary, it stated "all men are created free and equal"... The majority of the people of South Carolina, who are rapidly becoming property-holders, are colored citizens—the descendants of the African race—who have been ground down by three hundred years of degradation, and now that the opportunity is afforded, let them be protected by their political rights (Du Bois, 1935, p. 396).

After Randolph's address, the Convention banned discrimination based on race. The Convention then discussed the establishment of a public educational system.

Randolph began the discussion and included the following in a petition for public education: (a) that the Freedmen's Bureau continue its educational work until civil authority was restored in the state; (b) a provision to establish a Bureau of education so that an "efficient system of schools might be provided" (Taylor, 1924, p. 136).

Fundamental to Randolph's petition was his belief that the State's impoverished condition would prove to be a barrier to the establishment of a state supported system of free common schools. Some of Randolph's colleagues, including Legislator Alonzo J. Ransier, were not in total agreement with him. They moved expeditiously to create a state supported system of schools. Although Randolph felt that civil unrest and financial instability would prevent a state supported system from succeeding, he did not openly dissent. The state legislature, with blacks composing a majority in the lower house, then established an education article and made it a part of the State Constitution. It is important to note that Randolph was not only a Convention delegate, but also the Chairman of the Republican State executive committee. Randolph's position as Chairman may account for why he was able to voice his opinion in such a prominent manner.

The Educational Provision

Taylor and Du Bois both indicated that the educational provision was a major topic at the Convention. The provision provided for universal and free education, as well as the co-education of both blacks and whites at all public educational institutions. The system of education was to be financed by an annual legislative tax on real estate and a one-dollar poll tax on each adult male in South Carolina. However, the poll tax was not included in the Constitution and therefore was unenforceable. The following is a list of results of the educational provision: (a) the creation of the State Board of Education with a State Superintendent and County school commissioners, (b) the maintenance of a state university, and (c) the separation of the church from any control of the school system and its funds (Taylor, 1924, p. 99).

There was no clear explanation for why legislators deliberately separated education from the church, particularly since Randolph and others were religious men. However, the fact that they did this suggested that legislators firmly believed that public education was a matter of State that religious organizations should not control.

According to the *Charleston Daily Courier*, a considerable debate arose over the idea of including the term "compulsory" in the Constitution. After a period of discussion on the education issue, it was proposed that there should be compulsory attendance of all children between the ages of 6 and 16. The following appeared in the March 4, 1868 issue of the paper referring to compulsory attendance at state schools:

> This gave rise to a sharp and animated debate, in which it was argued by those in favor of striking out the word compulsory, that it would appear to be the intention of the committee to force the white and colored children to attend the same school (p. 5).

Charles P. Leslie, a white legislator, who had involved himself in the debate, stated to the Convention that an educational provision using the word "compulsory" would never be enforced. The Convention adjourned for the day shortly thereafter.

The New York Times also reported on the Convention proceedings of March 3. In a brief update of the proceedings also appearing on March 4, 1868, the newspaper declared that "an attempt was made by a strong faction to force colored children into schools and colleges among the whites" (p. 4). *The New York Times* may have been referring to black legislators when it used the term "faction".

On March 4, the Convention met again and began the day by discussing the education issue. Francis L. Cardozo spoke on the compulsory clause at length, almost as if to clarify or explain the rationale behind it. Cardozo stated that the term "compulsory" was not meant to imply that whites would be forced to attend schools with blacks, but was to insure that black parents would support education. Cardozo stated that a compulsory clause in the constitution would not only facilitate black education, but make it difficult for opponents to deny blacks the right to education. In spite of Cardozo's explanation, legislators decided not to include the term "compulsory" in the Constitution and settled to first organize a system of schools open to both races before considering such a feature.[10]

Article 10

The educational provision of the Convention was referred to as Article 10 of the South Carolina Constitution. It was composed of eleven sections and was declared on Saturday, March 14, 1868, after fifty-one sessions.

In addition to its openness to both races, two other significant points made by the education article were that education would be universal and free. Blacks would have the right to attend both grade schools and institutions of higher education along with whites.

---

[10] (*Charleston Daily Courier*, 5 March 1868).

Many white leaders opposed the mixing of races. Former Freedmen's Bureau leader and then Convention Legislator Robert K. Scott, was one of them. He concluded at the Convention that mixed race schools would drive whites out of the system. Scott became Governor of South Carolina in July of 1868 (Taylor, 1924, p. 166).

There were some whites that were more compassionate than Governor Scott. Justus Jillison, an educator from Massachusetts, who served the Freedmen's Bureau in South Carolina, believed that black children deserved the right to attend free and equal schools simply by citizenship. Jillison was a supporter of mixed schools and was elected to the position of State Superintendent of Education in July at the first election held after the 1868 Convention (Williamson, 1965, p. 221).

Although black leaders unanimously supported Article 10, some prominent legislators felt that it was unlikely that blacks or whites would immediately support mixed race schools because of the racial division in the state. Francis L. Cardozo, who served as chairman of the Education Committee at the Convention, and Jonathan Jasper Wright, were among them.

Equally as significant as the co-education of the races, was the fact that Article 10 would require the state to bear the burden of supporting the new educational system. The state government would have to secure educational funds and allocate them properly. The impoverished condition of the state ensured that securing funds would be very difficult. Uncertainty as to how to administer funds also proved to be problematic.

<u>The Death of Benjamin Franklin Randolph</u>

Racial hostility intensified between the races after the controversial requirements of Article 10 and the new constitution. Randolph, who began the discussion that led to the creation of the article, fell victim to this type of hostility. He was killed in November of 1868 while canvassing South Carolina on behalf of the Republican Party. It was believed that the Ku Klux Klan murdered Randolph because he was an outspoken black leader. (Taylor, 1924, p. 188).

It is important to identify two theories concerning Randolph's death. First, Taylor (1924) linked the deaths of Randolph and other black leaders to the Ku Klux Klan as acts of political intimidation. Second, Holt (1977) suggested that members of the Republican Party, who disagreed with a black man serving as Chairman of the executive committee, might have been responsible (p. 105).

Barriers that Affected the Educational Provision

In 1871, a report by Justus Jillison on the progress of education was made public. The report indicated that universal and free education without racial distinction was not successful from 1868 to 1871. According to the Jillison Report, three barriers affected the success of the educational provision of the 1868 Convention. The first barrier that affected the success of South Carolina's first constitutional public school system was the financial condition of the state. Scarce resources led to inadequate funding for the educational system. Taylor noted that the following two facts insured that the educational system would not be properly funded: (a) the Legislature only appropriated $50,000 for the system (an adequate amount would have been at least $500,000), (b) the poll tax, which was to support the system, went unpaid, and there was no penalty attached for non-payment (Taylor, 1924, p. 99).

The second barrier was that the Superintendent was given no real power to act. As Superintendent, Jillison was given no jurisdiction, supervisory, or discretionary power. Further, since both the Superintendent and County School Commissioners were elected by popular vote, the Superintendent was only a distributor of state school funds to the Commissioners. After the Superintendent distributed funds to the Commissioners (who led specified districts without the Superintendent having any real power over their jurisdictions), he had no constitutional power to control how those funds were used (Taylor, 1924, p. 100).

The third barrier that affected the success of the educational provision was racial hostility. Whites were openly hostile towards blacks after the war. Although there was resentment from both whites and blacks, blacks were more willing than whites to be educated in mixed raced schools. Even poor whites thought it beneath them to learn with blacks. In general, whites simply would not cooperate with racially mixed schools (Taylor, 1924, p. 101).

The former landed aristocracy had the true power to block racial mixed schools. They resented black governance and used their cohesion and resources to do so. This was clearly stated by Taylor (1924):

> A third, and perhaps most significant consideration was found in that little or no genuine interest in the success of public free education could be engendered. The former ruling class had refused political cooperation with blacks, which, from the point of view of voting power, were now dominant. The former were, moreover, never committed to a system of statewide free education and they were not now likely to favor any constructive movement that might redound to the credit of the reconstruction government. Besides they were bitterly opposed to the co-

education of blacks and whites. From this source, therefore, there could be expected no real assistance (p. 101).

Black Leadership during Reconstruction

South Carolina Reconstruction included the majority presence of black legislators in state government. Supported by the black vote, a majority of blacks served in the lower house of the Reconstruction legislature from 1868 to 1871. Holt (1977) recorded that the House of Representatives was composed of 75 blacks and 49 whites; 86 of the 155 members of the House of Representatives and Senate were black from 1868 to 1869. From 1870 to 1871, 89 out of 158 of the total number of legislators was black. All of the black legislators were Republican (p. 97).

Blacks were visible as well as prominent in the legislature during the early years of Reconstruction. Two blacks served as Lieutenant Governor, Alonzo J. Ransier, 1870 to 1872 and Richard H. Gleaves, 1872 to 1876. Samuel J. Lee served as Speaker of the House from 1872 to 1874. In reference to the legislative success of black Republicans, Holt (1977) wrote the following:

> In almost every legislative session black Republicans were much more successful on legislative roll calls than their white counterparts. During the ten sessions the South Carolina House of Representatives held between 1868 and 1876, black legislators had an average collective success ratio of 33, while white Republicans scored only 22 (p. 100).

Significant legislation was adopted by South Carolina under the leadership of a majority black legislature. In addition to the adoption of a state supported system of education and a state policy on suffrage, other important decisions were made. Blacks were influential in the establishment of governmental term limits, marriage laws and the role of the State Supreme Court (Taylor, 1924, p. 128).

Black Legislators

The fact that many of the black legislators had been slaves or had little education led to the misconception that all black legislators were ignorant or illiterate. On the contrary, Holt (1977) claimed that most of the black legislators elected to office between 1868 and 1876 had been free even before the Civil War, and were generally well educated for that time (p. 43). He wrote the following statement in reference to the black legislators:

> The overwhelming majority (65 percent) was literate, and one-tenth was professionally or college-trained. Of those whose pre-war occupations can be identified, both the freedmen and freeborn were drawn heavily from among the artisan class. However, among post-war occupations professionals constituted the largest single category. Ministers and teachers predominated among the professionals (76 percent) but ten of these lawmakers, were, or became, lawyers during their terms of office (p. 38).

One of those individuals was Francis L. Cardozo. Cardozo was born free and was of black, Jewish and Indian descent. He was educated at the University of Glasgow and in London. Cardozo served as a Presbyterian minister and was Principal of Avery Institute in Charleston after the war. Cardozo also served as Secretary of State from 1868-1872 and Treasurer of the State from 1872-1876 (McCarthy, 1999, p. 376).

Jonathan Jasper Wright was another black legislator who was well trained and educated. Born in Luzerne County, Pennsylvania, Wright attended Lancasterian

University in Ithaca, New York. He also studied law in several Pennsylvania offices and was the first black person to be admitted to the State bar. In South Carolina, Wright served with the AMA and later with the Republican Party. Politically active for most of his time in South Carolina, Wright was appointed to the State Supreme Court in February 1870, by the general assembly. Wright's appointment to the South Carolina State Supreme Court represented the first time in history that a black person sat on the Supreme Court of any American state (Hine, 1999, p. 34). Randolph, the subject of this thesis, was also well trained and educated. Ironically, Cardozo, Wright, and Randolph served with the AMA in 1865, prior to becoming "prominent officeholders" in South Carolina (Holt, 1977, p. 81).

Regarding the character of black legislators, Du Bois (1935) stated that they were viewed by northerners as superior in ability and in decency, than most of the white legislators. Du Bois also noted that black legislators thought clearly and made sound decisions. According to Du Bois (1910), a high ranking white governmental official during Reconstruction, stated the following about Cardozo:

> I have never heard one word or seen one act of Mr. Cardozo's, which did not confirm my confidence in his personal integrity, in his political honor and zeal for the honest administration of the State Government. On every occasion, and under all circumstances, he has been against fraud and jobbery, and in favor of good measures and good men (p. 797).

The prominence of Cardozo was confirmed by an article that appeared in the June 22, 1874 issue of the *New York Times*. Cardozo was interviewed by an unnamed correspondent of the newspaper about the division between Democrats and Republicans in South Carolina. At the time of the interview, Cardozo was the State Treasurer and a Republican. The correspondent referred to Cardozo as one of the most prominent black leaders in the South.

Cardozo believed that from 1868 to 1872 the most significant issue that contributed to the division between Democrats and Republicans was the misuse of financial resources. He stated,

> In the misadministration of the state previous to 1872 the chief difficulties had been of a financial nature—the large issue of bonds, and the loose method of collecting taxes, and the still looser method of dispersing them when collected (p. 1).

This misuse of funds also led to corruption. Cardozo further indicated that Democrats connected the black Republican legislators to corruption and the problems that occurred. However, Cardozo believed that black legislators were not completely to blame for the problems. He indicated that blacks did not directly make the decisions that led to the misuse of government resources. Cardozo concluded that a few leading Democrats were determined to oppose black legislators and magnify the mistakes that were made when they were in office. The correspondent wrote,

> The crimes and mistakes committed by the Republicans of South Carolina had been very serious ones, but the Democracy, instead of trying to correct them, had done everything to augment and increase them. Mr. Cardozo believed that the masses of the Democratic party in the state—particularly the young men—had but little sympathy with those who controlled them politically; but so powerful was

the influence of a few leading spirits that they dominated over the others, who had

not the moral courage to resist them (p. 5).

Cardozo made no mention in this interview of a major internal conflict between blacks and whites within the Republican Party. Notably, Holt (1977) suggested that there was indeed a significant conflict within the Republican Party between 1868 and 1876. He held that both black and white Republicans failed to keep the party united and specifically pointed to a division between black political leaders. Holt claimed that the black political leaders (mostly mulattoes) who had been free during the antebellum period often expressed different views than those that had been enslaved (p. 58).

Blacks actively participated in state government until their presence began to diminish there in the late 1870's. Intimidation and threats had deterred blacks from voting widely. During the 1880's, poor whites became politically active and with the influence of such men as Benjamin R. Tillman, who served the state as Governor from 1890 to 1894, they aggressively opposed black equality. By 1895, a new constitution had been framed that prevented most blacks from voting and prevented all blacks from holding political positions (Taylor, 1924, p. 313).

The Benefits of Reconstruction

In spite of the movement that opposed and forced blacks out of government, black legislators helped South Carolina through the difficult period of Reconstruction. The framing of a new constitution was one of the watershed events of this transitional period. The Constitution of 1868 included for the first time in the history of South Carolina, an educational provision (Vaughn, 1974, p. 51). Even though some historians viewed black suffrage and participation in government as an incredible mistake, Du Bois (1910) pointed to three benefits of Reconstruction: (a) democratic government, (b) free public schools, (c) new social legislation (p. 795). Du Bois (1910) claimed that the Constitution also demonstrated the fact that South Carolina had integrated democratic principles, characterized by the inclusion of the best interest of all citizens, into State law. The creation of public highways, universal suffrage and a public school system were examples of major efforts towards democracy. Du Bois (1910) wrote,

> The Constitution of 1868, on the other hand, was a modern democratic document starting (in marked contrast to the old constitutions) with a declaration that "We, the People", framed it and preceded by a broad Declaration of Rights which did away with property qualifications and based representation directly on population instead of property (p. 795).

A new penal system and the establishment of charitable organizations were also made a part of the Constitution. Even though after only a decade opponents of the Republican led Reconstruction legislature had assumed political power, the Constitution was only slightly modified. South Carolina's 1868 Constitution remained unchanged for 27 years (Du Bois, 1910, p. 799).

The 1868 Constitutional Convention of South Carolina began a new but short lived era for blacks. The brief period of equality after the Convention allowed many blacks to realize the right to such things as suffrage and public education, which had been denied to blacks for decades. Although Randolph was killed less than a year after the Convention, other black leaders continued to be involved in political affairs as representatives of the black population.

CONCLUSION

With this thesis, I have attempted to demonstrate how blacks in South Carolina pursued the creation of schools to improve their condition after the Civil War. They began this pursuit without the support of prevailing state laws and continued until State constitutional law supported them. I have proposed that before Reconstruction, an educational provision for a state supported public school system did not exist in South Carolina's Constitution. However, in 1868 the South Carolina legislature placed into the constitutional law an education article, which mandated the equal access to public education for both blacks and whites. Randolph was noteworthy in this process.

I began research on this thesis because I was interested in learning more about Randolph and his participation in South Carolina, but I had no idea what additional facts or theories would emerge. I found that Randolph and other black leaders were active and directly involved in several important issues during the early years of Reconstruction in South Carolina. My investigation into Randolph and his efforts led me to discover the importance of other black leaders in South Carolina during this time. I then chose to learn more about the early beginnings of education in South Carolina.

I have asserted that in practice, education was not successful from 1868 to 1871, based on Justis Jillison's 1871 education report, and I discussed the barriers that affected the development of the state, as well as the success of the educational provision.

The notion that racial division prevented the initial success of education was confirmed. However, my research also revealed that a significant political battle between Democrats and Republicans existed in South Carolina. The controversy that existed was based on race and opposition against blacks participating as leaders in state government. The political division between Democrats and Republicans may begin to provide an explanation for why black legislators were blamed for the problems of Reconstruction and why their significance has been discredited. Although it was proposed that the former landed aristocracy became politically powerful during Reconstruction and may have fostered the controversy, I was unable to conclude with my research that the former landed aristocracy was directly involved. I was able to find and incorporate into this thesis, a primary source reference (the 1874 *New York Times* interview with Cardozo) to support the significance of blacks as legislators and the existence of a significant struggle between Democrats and Republicans.

The goal of this thesis was to shed light on the participation of former slaves and black leaders in reconstituting South Carolina during Reconstruction. The results of my research confirmed that blacks and specifically black leaders were active and contributed to the adoption of education as a constitutional right for blacks in South Carolina.

REFERENCES

Allen, J.E. (1968). <u>The Negro in New York.</u> New York: Exposition Press.

Anderson, J.D. (1988). <u>The education of blacks in the south, 1860-1935.</u> Chapel Hill: The University of North Carolina Press.

Berlin, I.(Ed.). (1982). <u>Freedom: A documentary history of emancipation 1861-1867.</u> New York: Cambridge University Press.

Birnie, C.W. (1927). Education of the negro in Charleston, South Carolina, prior to the civil war. In <u>Journal of negro history, 11,</u> (p. 13). Washington: Association for the Study of Negro Life and History.

De Kiewiet, C. W. (1965). Book review. [Review of After Slavery: the Negro in South Carolina during Reconstruction]. <u>The Virginia Quarterly Review, 41,</u> (1), (p. 16).

Du Bois, W.E.B. (1910). <u>Black reconstruction and its benefits.</u> Washington, DC: American Historical Association.

_____. (1935). <u>Black reconstruction in America.</u> Philadelphia: Albeit Saifer.

Foner, P.S., & Walker, G.E. (1980). <u>Proceedings of the black state conventions 1840-1865.</u> Proceedings of the black state conventions 1840-1865, 2, 286-303.

Glashan, R. R. (1979). <u>American governors and gubernatorial elections, 1775-1978.</u> Westport, CT: Meckler Books.

Glymph, T. (1998). Book review. [Review of A Hard Fight for We]. <u>The journal of american history, 85,</u> (3), 1082-1083.

Hamilton, D. W. (1999). Benjamin Franklin Randolph. In American national biography, 18, (p. 121). New York: Oxford University Press.

Hine, W.C. (1999). Johnathan Jasper Wright. In American national biography, 24, (p. 34). New York: Oxford University Press.

Holt, T. C. (1977). Black over white: Negro political leadership in South Carolina during Reconstruction. Chicago: University of Illinois.

Johnson, E. D. (1965). Book review. [Review of After Slavery: the Negro in South Carolina during Reconstruction]. Library journal, 90, (9), (p. 2261)

Jones, J. (1980). Soldiers of light and love: Northern teachers and Georgia blacks. Chapel Hill: The University of North Carolina Press.

Lewis, D. L. (2000). W.E.B. Du Bois: The fight for equality and the American century, 1919-1963. New York: Holt and Company.

Logan, R. W. (1936). Book review. [Review of Black Reconstruction]. Journal of negro history, 1936, 61-62.

McCarthy, T.P. (1999). Francis L. Cardozo. In American national biography, 4, (p. 376). New York: Oxford University Press.

Morris, R. C. (1973). Reading, riting, and reconstruction. Chicago: University of Chicago.

Ovington, M. W. (1925). Book chat. [Review of The Negro in South Carolina During Reconstruction]. Amsterdam news, 16, (33), p. 16, Col. 6-7.

Perman, M. (1978). Book review. [Review of Black over White: Negro Political Leadership in South Carolina during Reconstruction]. American historical review, 80, (1), (p. 812).

Rousseve, C. B. (1937). The negro in Louisiana aspects of his history and his literature. New Orleans: Xavier University Press.

Schwalm, L. A. (1997). A hard fight for we: women's transition from slavery to freedom in South Carolina. Urbana: University of Illinois Press.

Taylor, A. A. (1924). The negro in South Carolina during the reconstruction. New York: AMS Press.

Vaughn, W. P. (1974). Schools for all: The blacks and public education in the south, 1865-1877. Lexington: The University Press of Kentucky.

Vicary, E. Z. (1999). Daniel Alexander Payne. In American national biography, 17, (p.170). New York: Oxford University Press.

Wesley, C.H. (1926). Negro labor in the United States 1850-1925. New York: Vanguard Press.

Wesley, C. H. (1935). Book review. [Review of Black Reconstruction Propaganda and historical writing: The emancipation of the historian opportunity]. A journal of negro life, 13, (8), p. 244.

Williamson, J. (1965). After slavery: The negro in South Carolina during reconstruction, 1861-1877. Durham, NC: The University of North Carolina.

Woodruff, J. (1868). Proceedings of the constitutional convention of South Carolina, 1868. New York: Arno Press.

Woodson, C. G. (1918). A century of Negro migration. Washington: Association for the Study of Negro Life and History.

www.ingramcontent.com/pod-product-compliance
Lightning Source LLC
Chambersburg PA
CBHW031421040426
42444CB00005B/668